THE COACHING JOURNEY OF ENZO MARESCA

The Life and Career, Trophy Cabinet, Tactics, style of play of the Manager and why he is a perfect fit for the blues project

By

Jim Wilson

Copyright © 2024 Jim Wilson

All rights reserved. No part of this publication may be reproduced, distributed, or transmitted in any form or by any means, including photocopying, recording, or other electronic or mechanical methods, without the prior written permission of the publisher, except in the case of brief quotations embodied in critical reviews and certain other noncommercial uses permitted by copyright law

Table of contents

Foreword   **7**

    Introduction to Enzo Maresca's Influence on
Football   8

Chapter 1: Early Life and Playing Career   **13**

    Childhood and Early Influences   13

    Professional Debut and Career Highlights   14

    Transition from Player to Coach   15

Chapter 2: The Coaching Journey   **17**

    Initial Coaching Roles and Experiences   17

    Key Learning from Working with Pep Guardiola at
Manchester City   18

    Managerial Stints and Growth   20

**Chapter 3: Leicester City and Championship
Triumph**   **23**

    Appointment and Objectives   23

    Building the Team: Key Players and Strategies   24

        Key Players   24

        Strategies: 25

    Path to the Championship Title   26

    Key Phases of the Season: 27

    Achievements: 28

Chapter 4: Managerial Style and Philosophy   **29**

    Tactical Principles and Formations   29

        Possession-Based Football: 29

        High Pressing: 30

        Fluid Formations: 30

Key Tactical Elements:	31
Training Methods and Player Development	31
Influence of Mentors and Personal Evolution	33
Pep Guardiola:	34
Manuel Pellegrini:	34
Playing Career:	34
Personal Evolution:	35
Breakdown of Defensive and Offensive Systems	37
Defensive Systems:	37
Adaptations and In-Game Management	43
Chapter 6: Key Matches and Tactical Mastery	**45**
Analysis of Pivotal Games at Leicester City	45
1. Leicester City vs. Norwich City (3-1)	45
2. Leicester City vs. Watford (2-0)	47
Detailed Case Studies of Tactical Implementations	48
Successes and Learning Points from Critical Matches	51
Successes:	51
Learning Points:	52
Chapter 7: Achievements and Trophies	**55**
Complete List of Managerial Accolades	55
In-Depth Look at Significant Milestones	56
Personal Reflections on Successes	58
Chapter 8: The Chelsea Project	**61**
Background on Chelsea's Vision and Goals	61
Reasons for Maresca's Suitability for Chelsea	62
Tactical Alignment	63
Youth Development	64

Leadership Qualities	65
Innovation and Adaptability	65
Experience with Elite Clubs	66
Success Under Pressure	66
Player Relationships	67
Long-Term Vision	68
Cultural Fit	68
Chapter 9: Challenges and Future Prospects	**71**
Potential Obstacles at Chelsea	71
Strategies for Overcoming Challenges	73
Long-Term Goals and Ambitions	75
Chapter 10: Legacy and Impact	**79**
Influence on Modern Football Tactics	79
Contributions to Coaching and Mentorship	79
Lasting Legacy in the Football World	81
Appendix	**85**
Statistics and Records	85

Foreword

Foreword

Football is constantly evolving, with each generation bringing new skills, creativity, and leadership. Among the contemporary figures influencing this dynamic scene, Enzo Maresca stands out as a remarkable individual whose journey from professional player to respected coach exemplifies persistence, resourcefulness, and an enduring love for the beautiful game. This book dives into Enzo Maresca's life and career, following him from the lively streets of Pontecagnano Faiano, Italy, to his legendary managing position at Leicester City and beyond. As we investigate his past, we discover the attributes and principles that have not only characterized his career but also left an indelible imprint on the teams he has led and the players he has mentored.

By examining Maresca's influence on football, we aim to provide readers with a comprehensive understanding of his contributions to the sport. His tactical acumen, his approach to player development, and his success in various managerial roles are all testament to his profound impact.

This foreword sets the stage for an in-depth journey into the life of a man who continues to inspire through his dedication to football, his innovative strategies, and his ability to lead with both vision and heart.

Introduction to Enzo Maresca's Influence on Football

Enzo Maresca's influence on football is multifaceted, spanning his achievements as a player, his tactical innovations as a coach, and his role in nurturing young talent. Born on February 10, 1980, in Pontecagnano Faiano, Italy, Maresca's early years were marked by a deep love for football, which propelled him into the professional realm at a young age.

As a player, Maresca's career took him across several top leagues in Europe, including Serie A, La Liga, and the English Premier League. His versatility as a midfielder, coupled with his technical skills and strategic understanding of the game, earned him recognition and respect. Playing for clubs like Juventus, Fiorentina, Sevilla, and West Bromwich Albion, Maresca demonstrated a keen tactical awareness that would later become a hallmark of his coaching style.

Maresca's transition from player to coach was seamless, driven by his inherent understanding of the game's intricacies. His coaching philosophy is deeply rooted in the principles he absorbed during his playing days and his time as an assistant under Pep Guardiola at Manchester City. Guardiola's influence is evident in Maresca's emphasis on possession-based football, high pressing, and fluid attacking play.

At Manchester City, Maresca honed his skills as a tactician, contributing to the development of the club's playing style and the success of its youth teams. His ability to blend strategic planning with player-centric coaching has been a defining feature of his career. This approach was prominently displayed during his tenure at

Parma and later at Leicester City, where he led the team to the Championship title, showcasing his capacity to adapt and thrive in diverse footballing environments.

Maresca's influence extends beyond his immediate managerial successes. He is known for his commitment to developing young talent, and fostering a culture of growth and learning within his teams. His work with young players has not only enhanced their skills but also prepared them for the demands of professional football. This dedication to youth development is aligned with the modern football ethos, which values the integration of academy products into the first team.

Moreover, Maresca's tactical innovations have left a lasting impact on the teams he has managed. His preference for dynamic, attacking football has provided a refreshing contrast to more conservative approaches, making his teams both effective and entertaining to watch. His ability to implement complex tactical systems while maintaining team cohesion and morale speaks to his exceptional leadership qualities.

Enzo Maresca's influence on football is profound and far-reaching. His journey from a talented midfielder to a visionary coach illustrates the power of passion, innovation, and dedication. As we delve deeper into his life and career in this book, we will uncover the strategies, philosophies, and personal attributes that make Maresca a significant figure in the world of football, and a perfect fit for ambitious projects like that of Chelsea.

Early Life and Playing Career

Chapter 1: Early Life and Playing Career

Childhood and Early Influences

Enzo Maresca was born on February 10, 1980, in Pontecagnano Faiano, a small town in the province of Salerno, Italy. Growing up in a football-loving nation, Maresca was naturally drawn to the sport from a young age. His early years were characterized by an unyielding passion for football, which he nurtured by playing in the streets and local pitches of his hometown.

Maresca's family played a significant role in his early development. His father, a devoted football enthusiast, often took him to local matches, instilling in him a deep love for the game. Additionally, his mother's support was instrumental in balancing his budding football career with his education. These early influences provided Maresca with a solid foundation, both technically and mentally, to pursue a career in professional football.

Professional Debut and Career Highlights

Maresca's professional journey began when he joined the youth academy of AC Milan, one of Italy's premier football clubs. His technical skills and tactical awareness quickly set him apart, leading to his professional debut with West Bromwich Albion in the English Premier League during the 1998-1999 season. Despite his young age, Maresca demonstrated remarkable maturity and versatility on the pitch.

His performances caught the attention of several top-tier clubs, and in 2000, he signed with Juventus, one of Italy's most storied clubs. At Juventus, Maresca honed his skills further under the guidance of experienced teammates and coaches. His tenure at Juventus included notable performances in Serie A and European competitions, showcasing his ability to perform at the highest levels of football.

After Juventus, Maresca's career saw him traverse various leagues and clubs, each stint adding a new dimension to his playing style. He played for clubs such as Bologna,

Piacenza, Fiorentina, and Sevilla. His time at Sevilla was particularly distinguished; he became a fan favorite for his pivotal role in the midfield and helped the club secure multiple titles, including two UEFA Cups in 2006 and 2007. These achievements cemented his reputation as a dependable and skilled midfielder.

Transition from Player to Coach

Maresca's transition from player to coach was a natural progression, driven by his deep understanding of the game and his desire to remain connected to football. After retiring as a player in 2017, he began to pursue coaching certifications, earning his UEFA Pro License. His first major coaching role came as an assistant to Manuel Pellegrini at West Ham United, where he gained invaluable insights into the managerial aspects of football.

Maresca's coaching career took a significant turn when he joined Manchester City as an assistant coach under Pep Guardiola. Working with Guardiola, one of the most respected managers in modern football, profoundly influenced Maresca's tactical philosophies and coaching methods. He was heavily involved in the development of Manchester City's playing style and contributed to the success of the club's youth teams.

In 2021, Maresca was appointed as the head coach of Parma in Serie B, demonstrating his readiness to take on more substantial challenges. His tenure at Parma, although brief, provided him with the experience and confidence needed to manage a first team. He then moved to Leicester City, where he led the team to the Championship title, showcasing his tactical prowess and leadership abilities.

Now, as the newly appointed manager of Chelsea, Maresca brings a wealth of experience, a proven track record, and a fresh, innovative approach to Stamford Bridge. His journey from a passionate young footballer in Italy to a respected manager in the Premier League is a testament to his dedication, skill, and unwavering love for the game.

Chapter 2: The Coaching Journey

Initial Coaching Roles and Experiences

After hanging up his boots in 2017, Enzo Maresca swiftly transitioned into coaching, leveraging his extensive playing experience and tactical knowledge. His first significant role came as an assistant coach under Manuel Pellegrini at West Ham United. This position allowed Maresca to delve into the tactical and operational aspects of coaching at a high level. Working alongside Pellegrini, he gained insights into match preparation, player management, and the intricate details of game strategy. This foundational experience was crucial in shaping his approach to coaching.

Maresca's responsibilities at West Ham included assisting with training sessions, developing game plans, and analyzing opponents. His analytical mind and ability to convey complex tactical concepts to players made him a valued member of the coaching staff. This period was instrumental in building his confidence and understanding of the managerial side of football, preparing him for more prominent roles in the future.

Key Learning from Working with Pep Guardiola at Manchester City

In 2020, Maresca joined Manchester City as the head coach of the Elite Development Squad (EDS), a role that placed him under the mentorship of Pep Guardiola. This opportunity was a turning point in Maresca's coaching career. Guardiola, renowned for his innovative tactics and strategic brilliance, had a profound influence on Maresca's coaching philosophy.

Working closely with Guardiola, Maresca absorbed key aspects of the high-pressing, possession-based style that has become synonymous with Guardiola's teams. He learned the importance of positional play (or "Juego de posición"), which emphasizes maintaining team structure and creating numerical advantages across different zones of the pitch. This approach not only improves ball retention but also enhances the team's ability to control the game and create scoring opportunities.

Maresca also benefited from Guardiola's meticulous approach to preparation and his emphasis on continuous improvement. He observed how Guardiola tailored training sessions to address specific tactical scenarios and individual player development needs. This experience reinforced the importance of adaptability and innovation in coaching, elements that Maresca would later incorporate into his managerial style.

One of the significant takeaways from his time at Manchester City was the value of integrating youth players into the first team. Maresca played a pivotal role in developing young talents, some of whom graduated to the senior squad. His success with the EDS highlighted his ability to nurture and elevate young prospects, a trait highly regarded in modern football.

Managerial Stints and Growth

Maresca's first major managerial role came in 2021 when he was appointed head coach of Parma in Serie B. Although his tenure was short-lived, it provided valuable experience in managing a first team. At Parma, Maresca attempted to implement the progressive tactics he had honed under Guardiola, focusing on building from the back and controlling possession. Despite facing challenges, including injuries and inconsistent performances, Maresca's stint at Parma was a crucial learning experience, teaching him about the pressures and complexities of head coaching at a competitive level.

In 2022, Maresca took on the managerial role at Leicester City, a position that would significantly bolster his reputation. His appointment came at a critical time for the club, which was aiming for promotion to the Premier League. Maresca's impact was immediate and profound. He instilled a disciplined, attacking style of play that revitalized the team. His emphasis on tactical flexibility, player development, and high-intensity training sessions transformed Leicester into a formidable force in the Championship.

Under his guidance, Leicester City secured the Championship title, marking a major achievement in Maresca's managerial career.

His success was attributed to his ability to blend experienced players with emerging talents, fostering a cohesive and motivated squad. Key matches during this period showcased his tactical acumen, particularly in adapting game plans to exploit opponents' weaknesses and maximize his team's strengths.

Now, as the newly appointed manager of Chelsea, Maresca brings a wealth of experience and a proven track record of success.

His journey through various coaching roles and his mentorship under one of the game's greatest tacticians have equipped him with the skills and knowledge necessary to thrive at Stamford Bridge.

Maresca's coaching journey is a testament to his dedication, strategic brilliance, and unwavering passion for football.

Chapter 3: Leicester City and Championship Triumph

Appointment and Objectives

Enzo Maresca was appointed as the head coach of Leicester City in June 2022, at a time when the club was grappling with the aftermath of relegation from the Premier League. His appointment came with high expectations, as the club's primary objective was an immediate return to the top tier of English football. The board sought a manager who could rebuild the team, instill a winning mentality, and implement a modern, attractive style of play that would not only bring results but also resonate with the fans.

Maresca's objectives were clear: secure promotion to the Premier League, develop a cohesive and competitive squad, and lay the groundwork for sustained success. His background, particularly his experience with Manchester City's Elite Development Squad and his brief tenure at

Parma, positioned him as a promising candidate to achieve these goals.

Building the Team: Key Players and StrategieS

Upon taking charge, Maresca conducted a thorough assessment of the existing squad, identifying key areas that required reinforcement. His strategy revolved around blending experienced players with emerging talents, ensuring a balanced and dynamic team capable of adapting to different challenges throughout the season.

Key Players

1. Kiernan Dewsbury-Hall: The young midfielder emerged as a pivotal figure under Maresca, showcasing his ability to control the tempo of the game and contribute both defensively and offensively.

2. Jamie Vardy: Despite his advancing age, Vardy's experience and goal-scoring prowess were invaluable. Maresca managed his fitness and utilized his skills in crucial moments.

3. Harvey Barnes: As one of the team's primary creative outlets, Barnes thrived under Maresca's system, contributing with goals and assists.

4. James Maddison: His vision and passing ability were crucial in breaking down defenses, making him a central figure in Maresca's tactical setup.

5. New Signings: Maresca also brought in new talent to address specific needs. Strategic acquisitions helped strengthen the squad's depth and provided a fresh impetus.

Strategies:

Maresca's tactical approach was heavily influenced by his time at Manchester City. He favored a possession-based style of play, emphasizing building from the back, maintaining high press, and controlling the game through fluid passing and movement. His strategies included:

- High Pressing: Maresca instilled a high-pressing game, ensuring that the team remained aggressive and proactive in winning back possession.

- **Formations:** Utilizing a flexible 4-3-3 or 4-2-3-1 formation, he adapted his tactics based on the opposition, allowing the team to exploit weaknesses effectively.

- **Youth Integration:** Emphasizing the development of young players, Maresca gave several academy graduates significant playing time, fostering a culture of growth and learning.

Path to the Championship Title

The journey to the Championship title was marked by consistent performances, strategic brilliance, and a resilient squad that embraced Maresca's vision. The season began with a strong start, as Leicester quickly established themselves as title contenders. The team's ability to maintain possession and control games saw them dominate many matches, often overwhelming opponents with their high-intensity play.

Key Phases of the Season:

1. Strong Start: The opening months saw Leicester secure crucial victories, building momentum and confidence. The team's early dominance set the tone for the season, with Maresca's tactics being effectively implemented on the pitch.

2. Winter Resilience: The winter period tested the squad's depth and resilience. Injuries and fixture congestion posed challenges, but Maresca's rotation policy and tactical adjustments ensured the team remained competitive.

3. Critical Matches: Key victories against direct promotion rivals highlighted Leicester's credentials. Matches against teams like Norwich and Watford were particularly significant, showcasing the team's ability to perform under pressure.

4. Final Push: As the season neared its climax, Leicester's consistency paid off. The team secured important wins in the final stretch, ensuring their position at the top of the table.

Achievements:

- Promotion Secured: Leicester City clinched the Championship title with several games to spare, confirming their return to the Premier League.

- Statistical Success: The team boasted impressive statistics, including the highest possession percentage in the league, a testament to Maresca's tactical philosophy.

- Player Development: Several young players flourished under Maresca's guidance, establishing themselves as key members of the squad and contributing significantly to the team's success.

Enzo Maresca's tenure at Leicester City was a masterclass in effective management, strategic innovation, and inspirational leadership. His ability to rebuild a relegated team, implement a modern style of play, and secure promotion underscored his credentials as one of the most promising managers in football. As he now takes on the role of Chelsea's head coach, the lessons and successes from his time at Leicester will undoubtedly serve him well in his new challenge.

Chapter 4: Managerial Style and Philosophy

Tactical Principles and Formations

Enzo Maresca's tactical philosophy is heavily influenced by his time as a player and coach under some of the most esteemed figures in football. His approach is characterized by a commitment to possession-based football, high pressing, and fluid formations.

Possession-Based Football:

Maresca emphasizes maintaining control of the game through possession. This approach involves meticulous build-up play from the back, patient ball circulation, and exploiting spaces created by the opponent's defensive shape. His teams are trained to keep the ball and use it efficiently, prioritizing short, accurate passes and movement off the ball to create passing lanes.

High Pressing:

A cornerstone of Maresca's tactical approach is the high press. His teams are trained to aggressively press opponents high up the pitch, aiming to win back possession quickly and capitalize on the disorganization of the opposition. This tactic requires high levels of fitness, coordination, and a deep understanding of pressing triggers and positioning.

Fluid Formations:

Maresca often employs a 4-3-3 or 4-2-3-1 formation but is not rigid in his approach. His tactical flexibility allows for adjustments based on the opposition and game context. For example, he may switch to a 3-4-3 in certain phases of play to exploit the width and create overloads. This adaptability is a testament to his deep tactical understanding and ability to read the game.

Key Tactical Elements:

- **Positional Play:** Inspired by Pep Guardiola's "Juego de posición," Maresca emphasizes maintaining team structure and creating numerical advantages in specific areas of the pitch.

- **Building from the Back:** Goalkeepers and defenders are integral to the build-up play, initiating attacks with precise passing and movement to draw out opponents and create space.

- **Dynamic Wing Play:** Wingers and full-backs play crucial roles in stretching the field and providing width, often switching positions to disorient defenders.

Training Methods and Player Development

Maresca's training methods are comprehensive and designed to develop both the technical skills and tactical intelligence of his players. His sessions are meticulously planned to simulate match conditions and focus on specific aspects of the game.

Training Structure:

- Technical Drills Focus on ball control, passing accuracy, dribbling, and shooting. These drills are often performed at high intensity to replicate match pressure.

- Tactical Simulations: Small-sided games and positional drills are used to practice the team's tactical principles. These sessions emphasize positional awareness, movement off the ball, and decision-making under pressure.

- Fitness and Conditioning:Given the demands of a high-pressing game, physical conditioning is a crucial component. Fitness drills are integrated with ball work to ensure players are in peak physical condition while maintaining technical proficiency.

-Video Analysis: Maresca uses video analysis extensively to review matches, both for performance analysis and to study opponents. This helps players understand their roles within the tactical framework and learn from past performances.

Player Development:

Maresca is known for his ability to develop young talent. His approach to player development focuses on:

- Individualized Training: Tailoring training programs to address the specific needs and potential of each player.
- Mentorship: Providing guidance and feedback to help players improve their game understanding and technical skills.
- Promoting Youth: Giving young players opportunities to train with the first team and play in competitive matches, fostering their growth and integration into the senior squad.

Influence of Mentors and Personal Evolution

Enzo Maresca's managerial philosophy has been shaped significantly by his mentors and his evolution through various roles in football.

Pep Guardiola:

LoWorking under Pep Guardiola at Manchester City had a profound impact on Maresca. Guardiola's emphasis on positional play, his meticulous preparation, and his innovative tactics have all influenced Maresca's approach. Guardiola's ability to adapt his tactics based on the opposition and game context is a trait that Maresca has incorporated into his style.

Manuel Pellegrini:

During his time at West Ham United, Maresca learned the importance of calm and composed leadership from Manuel Pellegrini. Pellegrini's experience and his ability to manage diverse squads taught Maresca the value of maintaining harmony and morale within the team.

Playing Career:

Maresca's playing career across various leagues and under different managers provided him with a broad perspective on football tactics and management. His experiences in Italy, Spain, and England allowed him to integrate diverse tactical concepts and managerial styles into his philosophy.

Personal Evolution:

Maresca's journey from player to coach has been marked by continuous learning and adaptation. He has evolved from focusing primarily on tactical nuances to understanding the broader aspects of team management, player psychology, and long-term strategic planning. His adaptability and willingness to learn have been crucial in his development as a modern, forward-thinking manager.

Enzo Maresca's managerial style and philosophy are a blend of tactical innovation, rigorous training methods, and a deep commitment to player development. Influenced by his mentors and his extensive playing career, Maresca has developed a unique approach that emphasizes possession-based football, high pressing, and adaptability. As he embarks on his new challenge at Chelsea, these principles and experiences will be instrumental in shaping the club's future.

Detailed Analysis of Tactics

Chapter 5: Detailed Analysis of Tactics

Breakdown of Defensive and Offensive Systems

Defensive Systems:

Enzo Maresca's defensive strategies are characterized by organization, high pressing, and quick transitions. His approach emphasizes collective responsibility, with every player understanding their role in both defending and initiating attacks.

1. High Pressing:

 - Objective: To disrupt the opponent's build-up play and regain possession high up the pitch.

 - Execution: The team presses aggressively as a unit, often using a 4-3-3 or 4-2-3-1 formation. Forwards and attacking midfielders initiate the press, closing down passing lanes and forcing the opposition into mistakes.

 - Key Players: The wingers and central forward are crucial, using their speed and positioning to pressure the ball carriers. Central midfielders support by marking potential receivers and intercepting passes.

2. Defensive Organization:

- Objective: To maintain a compact shape and minimize space for the opposition.

- Execution:When pressing is bypassed, the team falls back into a structured defensive block. The full-backs tuck in to create a narrow back four, while midfielders drop to support and shield the defense. This ensures a solid central structure, forcing opponents wide where they are less dangerous.

-Key Players: Central defenders and a holding midfielder play critical roles in organizing the defense and intercepting passes.

3. Transition Defense:

-Objective: To quickly regain defensive shape and counter any fast breaks from the opposition.

-Execution: Upon losing possession, immediate pressure is applied to the ball carrier to delay the opponent's transition. Simultaneously, players sprint back to their defensive positions, ensuring the team is not caught out of shape.

- Key Players: The defensive midfielders and center-backs are vital in halting counter-attacks, often stepping up to break plays early.

Offensive Systems:

Maresca's offensive tactics are dynamic, relying on controlled possession, positional play, and quick, incisive passing to create goal-scoring opportunities.

1. Build-Up Play:

- Objective: To progress the ball methodically from the defense to the attack while maintaining possession.

- Execution: Goalkeepers and defenders are actively involved in starting attacks, using short passes to move the ball out from the back. Midfielders drop deep to provide passing options and help circulate the ball, creating triangles and diamonds for effective ball movement.

- Key Players: The center-backs, full-backs, and a deep-lying playmaker facilitate the build-up with their passing range and vision.

2. Positional Play:

- Objective: To create numerical advantages in different areas of the pitch and disrupt the opposition's defensive shape.

- Execution: Players maintain specific zones, ensuring width and depth in the attacking phase. Full-backs often advance high up the pitch to stretch the defense, while wingers cut inside to support the central attackers. Midfielders make forward runs to overload the opponent's defensive lines.

- Key Players: The attacking midfielders and wingers are crucial, using their movement and technical skills to exploit spaces between the lines.

3. Quick Transitions:

- Objective: To capitalize on the opponent's disorganization immediately after winning the ball.

- Execution:Upon regaining possession, the team quickly moves the ball forward through direct passes or dribbling. This fast transition aims to catch the opposition off guard and create goal-scoring opportunities before they can regroup defensively.

- Key Players: Quick and creative players like wingers and attacking midfielders are essential, as they can turn defensive actions into attacking plays with their speed and vision.

The use of technology and data in decision-making

Maresca advocates for integrating current technologies and data analytics to improve his tactical judgments and overall

1. Video Analysis:
   - Purpose: To provide detailed breakdowns of both team performances and individual player contributions.
   - Implementation: Matches are recorded and analyzed to identify strengths, weaknesses, and areas for improvement. This analysis is used to prepare for upcoming matches and develop specific tactical plans.
   - Outcome: Players receive tailored feedback, helping them understand their roles better and make informed adjustments to their play.

2. Data Analytics:

- Purpose: To gain insights into player performance, fitness levels, and tactical effectiveness.

- Implementation: Advanced metrics such as distance covered, pressing efficiency, passing accuracy, and positional heat maps are utilized. These data points help in making decisions about player selection, in-game adjustments, and long-term strategic planning.

- Outcome: Enhanced decision-making capabilities that lead to more effective training sessions, match preparation, and in-game tactics.

3. Wearable Technology:

- Purpose: To monitor and optimize player fitness and reduce the risk of injuries.

- Implementation: Players wear GPS trackers and heart rate monitors during training and matches. This data helps in managing workload, planning recovery, and tailoring fitness programs.

- Outcome: Improved player fitness, reduced injury rates, and optimal performance levels throughout the season.

Adaptations and In-Game Management

Maresca's ability to adapt his tactics and manage games effectively is a hallmark of his coaching prowess. He employs several strategies to ensure his team can respond to various match situations.

1. Tactical Flexibility:

- Approach: Maresca is not wedded to a single formation or style of play. He adapts his tactics based on the opposition, game context, and available personnel.

- Examples: Shifting from a 4-3-3 to a 3-4-3 to exploit wide areas or switching to a more defensive 4-2-3-1 when protecting a lead. His flexibility allows the team to remain unpredictable and versatile.

2. In-Game Adjustments:

- Approach: Maresca is proactive in making substitutions and tactical changes during matches to address emerging challenges or exploit new opportunities.

- Examples: Bringing on fresh legs to maintain pressing intensity, changing the formation to nullify an opponent's key player, or adjusting the team's attacking approach to break down a stubborn defense. These adjustments often turn the tide in crucial moments.

3. Player Instructions:

- Approach: Clear and concise communication with players ensures they understand their roles and responsibilities at all times.

- Examples: Issuing specific instructions to wingers to track back and help defensively or directing midfielders to push forward and support the attack. This level of detail helps maintain team cohesion and effectiveness.

Chapter 6: Key Matches and Tactical Mastery

Analysis of Pivotal Games at Leicester City

Enzo Maresca's tenure at Leicester City was marked by several key matches that showcased his tactical acumen and ability to adapt to different challenges. Here, we delve into some of these pivotal games, examining how Maresca's strategies played out on the field and the impact they had on Leicester's successful Championship campaign.

1. Leicester City vs. Norwich City (3-1)

- **Context:** This early-season match was crucial for setting the tone of Leicester's campaign. Norwich, a direct rival for promotion, posed a significant challenge.

- **Tactical Setup:** Maresca deployed a 4-3-3 formation, emphasizing high pressing and quick transitions.

- Key Strategies:

- High Press: From the kickoff, Leicester pressed aggressively, forcing Norwich into errors. This led to early turnovers and quick counter-attacks.

-Positional Play: The midfield trio of Dewsbury-Hall, Maddison, and Tielemans controlled the tempo, exploiting spaces between Norwich's lines.

- Wide Play: Wingers Harvey Barnes and Ademola Lookman stretched the defense, creating space for Vardy in the center.

- Outcome: Leicester's relentless pressure paid off, leading to an early goal. They maintained control throughout the match, and Maresca's tactical flexibility was evident as he switched to a more defensive 4-2-3-1 in the latter stages to secure the victory.

2. Leicester City vs. Watford (2-0)

- **Context**: Midway through the season, this match was critical to maintaining Leicester's position at the top of the table. Watford was known for its solid defensive setup and counter-attacking prowess.

- **Tactical Setup:** Maresca opted for a 3-4-3 formation to counter Watford's strengths and control the game.

- **Key Strategies:**

- Building from the Back: With three center-backs, Leicester confidently built play from the back, bypassing Watford's press.

- Midfield Dominance: The wing-backs pushed high up, creating numerical superiority in the midfield and allowing Maddison and Dewsbury-Hall to dictate play.

- Defensive Solidity: The three-man defense provided extra cover against Watford's counter-attacks.

- Outcome: Leicester's dominance in possession and well-organized defense nullified Watford's threat. The tactical switch to a 3-4-3 was a masterstroke, allowing Leicester to control the game and secure a vital win.

Detailed Case Studies of Tactical Implementations

1. Case Study: Defensive Adaptations Against Stoke City.

- Scenario: Facing a physical Stoke City team, known for their aerial threats and set-piece proficiency.

- Tactical Implementation:Maresca implemented a 4-1-4-1 formation to provide extra defensive cover.

- Defensive Shape:Ndidi played as a single pivot, dropping deep to shield the back four and intercept crosses.

- Aerial Dominance: Center-backs Soyuncu and Evans were tasked with winning aerial duels, while full-backs focused on closing down wide players to prevent crosses.

- Quick Counter-Attacks: Upon regaining possession, the team transitioned swiftly, utilizing the pace of wingers and Vardy to exploit the spaces left by Stoke's advanced players.

- Result: Leicester's disciplined defensive performance and effective counter-attacks resulted in a 1-0 victory, highlighting Maresca's ability to adapt his tactics to neutralize specific threats.

2. Case Study: Offensive Mastery Against Swansea City

- Scenario: Swansea City's compact defense required a tactical approach that could break down a well-organized backline.

- Tactical Implementation: Maresca employed a 4-2-3-1 formation with a focus on creative midfield play and overlapping full-backs.

- Creative Midfield: Maddison and Tielemans operated in advanced roles, providing key passes and creating scoring opportunities.

- Full-Back Involvement: Full-backs Ricardo Pereira and James Justin were instructed to overlap and deliver crosses into the box.

- Dynamic Movement: The front four interchanged positions frequently, confusing Swansea's defense.

- Result: The tactical approach led to a 3-0 victory, with Leicester breaking down Swansea's defense through intricate passing and well-timed runs. This match underscored Maresca's offensive ingenuity and ability to outthink defensive setups.

Successes and Learning Points from Critical Matches

Successes:

1. Consistency in High Press:

- Example: Throughout the season, Maresca's commitment to high pressing consistently disrupted opponents' build-up play. The success against Norwich was a prime example, where Leicester's high press led to multiple scoring opportunities and early goals.

- Learning Point: The high press, when executed with discipline and intensity, can be a game-changing strategy, especially against teams that struggle under pressure.

2. Adaptability in Formation:

- Example: The tactical switch to a 3-4-3 against Watford demonstrated Maresca's adaptability. By altering formations based on the opponent, he ensured that Leicester could exploit weaknesses and strengthen their defensive structure.

- Learning Point: Flexibility in tactics allows a team to be unpredictable and effectively counter varied opposition strategies.

Learning Points:

1. Handling Physical Teams:

- Example: The match against Stoke City highlighted the need for defensive robustness and aerial prowess. Leicester's preparation and tactical discipline were key to handling Stoke's physicality.

- Learning Point: Tailoring tactics to address the specific strengths of the opposition can neutralize their primary threats and secure vital points.

2. Breaking Down Compact Defenses:
- Example: The offensive strategy against Swansea, utilizing creative midfield play and overlapping full-backs, showed how to dismantle a compact defensive setup.

- **Learning Point:** Patience, creativity, and dynamic movement are essential to breaking down well-organized defenses, particularly in matches where the opponent sits deep.

Enzo Maresca's tenure at Leicester City provided numerous examples of tactical mastery and strategic thinking. His ability to analyze opponents, adapt his tactics, and implement effective strategies was instrumental in Leicester's Championship triumph. These key matches and tactical insights underscore the depth of Maresca's understanding of the game and his potential to succeed at the highest levels of football management.

Achievements and Trophies

Chapter 7: Achievements and Trophies

Complete List of Managerial Accolades

Enzo Maresca's managerial career, though relatively brief compared to some of his contemporaries, has been marked by significant achievements and accolades. Here is a comprehensive list of his managerial honors:

1. EFL Championship Title with Leicester City (2023-2024):
Leading Leicester City to the Championship title in his first full season in charge, securing promotion to the Premier League. This achievement highlighted Maresca's tactical prowess and ability to galvanize a team toward a common goal.

2. Manager of the Month Awards (Multiple):
Throughout the 2023-2024 season, Maresca received several Manager of the Month awards, recognizing his consistent performance and tactical ingenuity. These accolades underscored his ability to maintain high

standards over extended periods, adapting strategies to maintain Leicester's top position.

In-Depth Look at Significant Milestones

1. Appointment at Leicester City:

Maresca's appointment at Leicester City was a pivotal moment in his career. Tasked with returning the club to the Premier League, he embraced the challenge with innovative tactics and a clear vision for the team's future. His appointment brought a fresh perspective to Leicester, revitalizing the squad and implementing a dynamic, possession-based style of play that proved successful.

2. Championship Title Victory:

Securing the Championship title was a major milestone for Maresca. This achievement not only fulfilled the club's primary objective but also solidified his reputation as a competent and forward-thinking manager.

- Tactical Mastery: The title victory was built on a foundation of tactical versatility, with Maresca adeptly switching formations and strategies to outmaneuver opponents throughout the season. His use of a high press and quick transitions were particularly effective.

3. Development of Young Talent:

Maresca's commitment to developing young players was evident during his time at Leicester. He integrated several academy prospects into the first team, providing them with invaluable experience and fostering a culture of youth development.

This approach not only enhanced the team's depth but also ensured a sustainable future for the club, with young talents ready to step up and contribute at the highest level.

4. Tactical Innovation:

One of Maresca's significant milestones was his tactical innovation. Drawing on his experience with Pep Guardiola at Manchester City, he introduced a hybrid 3-4-3/4-3-3 system that allowed for fluid transitions between defense and attack. This flexibility made Leicester unpredictable and adaptable, capable of adjusting their play style to counter various opponents effectively.

5. Personal Growth and Learning:

Throughout his managerial journey, Maresca emphasized the importance of continuous learning and adaptation. His willingness to evolve his tactics and embrace new methodologies has been a cornerstone of his success.

This commitment to personal growth has enabled Maresca to remain at the forefront of modern football tactics, ensuring his teams are always well-prepared and competitive.

Personal Reflections on Successes

Enzo Maresca has often reflected on his successes with a sense of humility and a recognition of the collective effort involved. Here are some key reflections based on his public statements and interviews:

1. Emphasis on Team Effort:

Maresca frequently highlights the importance of the collective effort, acknowledging the contributions of his coaching staff, players, and the broader club infrastructure. He believes that success in football is never the result of one person but a unified team working towards a common goal.

2. Learning from Mentors:

He has expressed gratitude for the opportunities to learn from some of the best in the business, particularly Pep Guardiola. Maresca credits these experiences with shaping his tactical philosophy and managerial approach, emphasizing the value of mentorship in his development.

3. Adaptability and Innovation:

Reflecting on his tactical successes, Maresca often speaks about the need to adapt and innovate continually. He believes that staying ahead in football requires a willingness to embrace new ideas and methodologies, ensuring that his teams are always evolving.

4. Development of Players:

Maresca takes great pride in his role in developing young players. He sees this as a vital part of his job, not only for the immediate benefit of the team but also for the long-term health of the club. He has often remarked on the joy and satisfaction of seeing young talents thrive under his guidance.

5. Overcoming Challenges:

- Personal reflections also include the challenges faced and overcome. Maresca values the difficult moments as much as the triumphs, viewing them as critical learning experiences that have shaped his managerial career. He believes that adversity builds resilience and character, both essential qualities for sustained success in football.

Enzo Maresca's journey is a testament to his tactical intelligence, adaptability, and commitment to excellence. His achievements and milestones are not just personal victories but also reflect the success of the teams and individuals he has led and developed. As he continues to build on this foundation, his reflections provide valuable insights into the mindset and principles that drive his approach to football management.

Chapter 8: The Chelsea Project

Background on Chelsea's Vision and Goals

Chelsea Football Club, under the ownership of Todd Boehly and the management of its board, has been focusing on re-establishing itself as a dominant force in both English and European football. Following the departure of Mauricio Pochettino, the club aims to build a long-term project that combines immediate competitive success with sustainable growth and development. Key objectives include:

1. Winning Titles: Chelsea seeks to compete in the Premier League, Champions League, and domestic cups every season.

2. Youth Development: Integrating young talents from the academy into the first team, continuing the club's tradition of nurturing homegrown players.

3. Tactical Innovation: Implementing a modern, dynamic style of play that can adapt to the evolving landscape of football.

4. Global Brand Expansion: Enhancing the club's brand value through success on the pitch and strategic off-pitch initiatives.

Reasons for Maresca's Suitability for Chelsea

Enzo Maresca's suitability for the Chelsea managerial position stems from his combination of tactical acumen, player development focus, and experience at top clubs. His appointment aligns with Chelsea's vision for several reasons:

1. Proven Success: Leading Leicester City to the Championship title demonstrates his ability to achieve immediate success.

2. Tactical Flexibility: His tactical versatility allows him to adapt to various situations, a crucial trait for competing on multiple fronts.

3. Player Development: His track record of integrating young talents aligns with Chelsea's goal of promoting academy graduates.

4. Modern Approach: His modern, possession-based style of play fits Chelsea's aspiration for attractive football.

Tactical Alignment

Maresca's tactical philosophy includes several elements that align well with Chelsea's vision:

1. Possession-Based Play: Emphasizes controlling the game through possession, a style that Chelsea has often sought to implement.

2. High Press: Utilizes a high-pressing game to disrupt opponents' play, aligning with the club's desire for aggressive, front-foot football.

3. Versatility: Demonstrates tactical flexibility, switching between formations like 4-3-3 and 3-4-3, depending on the opposition and match context.

Youth Development

Maresca places significant emphasis on youth development, a critical aspect of Chelsea's strategy:

1. Academy Integration: Known for promoting young players to the first team, which is crucial for a club that prides itself on its academy.

2. Individual Growth: Focuses on individual player development, tailoring training to enhance each player's strengths and address weaknesses.

Leadership Qualities

Maresca's leadership qualities make him an ideal candidate for Chelsea:

1. Communication: Strong communicator who can effectively convey his vision and tactical instructions to players.

2. Inspirational: Known for his ability to inspire and motivate his team, fostering a winning mentality.

Innovation and Adaptability

Maresca's innovative approach and adaptability are vital for Chelsea's ambitions:

1. Embracing Technology: Utilizes modern technologies and data analysis to inform tactical decisions, aligning with Chelsea's advanced analytical approach.

2. Adaptive Tactics: Capable of adjusting tactics mid-game to respond to changing circumstances, ensuring that the team remains competitive.

Experience with Elite Clubs

Maresca's background with top-tier clubs like Manchester City provides valuable experience:

1. Elite Standards: Exposure to high standards of training and competition at Manchester City, which can be translated to Chelsea.

2. Learning from Guardiola: Gained insights from working under Pep Guardiola, one of the most successful managers in modern football.

Success Under Pressure

Maresca has demonstrated the ability to thrive under pressure:

1. Promotion Campaign: Successfully navigated the high-pressure environment of a promotion campaign with Leicester City.

2. Decisive Matches: Proven track record in crucial matches, showcasing his ability to manage and motivate the team when it matters most.

Player Relationships

Building strong relationships with players is one of Maresca's strengths:

1. Trust and Respect: Known for earning the trust and respect of his players through his approachability and understanding.

2. Development Focus: Prioritizes player development, fostering a supportive environment where players feel valued and motivated.

Long-Term Vision

Maresca's long-term vision aligns with Chelsea's goals:

1. Sustainable Success: Focuses on building a team that can achieve sustained success, balancing immediate results with long-term growth.

2. Club Identity: Aims to develop a team identity that is consistent with the club's values and aspirations.

Cultural Fit

Maresca's personality and managerial style make him a good cultural fit for Chelsea:

1. Professionalism: His professional approach aligns with Chelsea's standards of excellence.

2. Passion: Shares Chelsea's passion for football and commitment to achieving the highest levels of success.

Enzo Maresca's appointment as Chelsea's head coach is well-aligned with the club's vision and goals. His tactical acumen, focus on youth development, and experience with elite clubs make him a fitting choice to lead Chelsea into a new era of success.

Challenges and Future Prospects

Chapter 9: Challenges and Future Prospects

Potential Obstacles at Chelsea

Enzo Maresca, stepping into the role of Chelsea's head coach, will inevitably face several challenges that come with managing a top-tier club with high expectations. Here are some potential obstacles:

1. High Expectations and Pressure:

- Expectation for Immediate Success: Chelsea's history of frequent managerial changes and high standards means that Maresca will be under constant pressure to deliver immediate results in both domestic and European competitions.

- Scrutiny from Media and Fans: The intense scrutiny from the media and the passionate fan base can create a challenging environment, especially if results don't go according to plan early on.

2. Squad Management:

- Balancing a Large Squad: Managing a squad filled with high-profile players, including balancing playing time and managing egos, can be challenging. Chelsea's deep roster requires careful management to keep all players motivated and engaged.

- Injury Management: Ensuring key players remain fit throughout the season, given the physical demands of the Premier League and other competitions.

3. Transfer Market Challenges:

- Recruitment Strategy: Aligning transfer market activities with the club's long-term vision while navigating the complexities of the market.

- Financial Fair Play (FFP): Operating within the constraints of FFP regulations, which may limit spending and necessitate strategic planning.

4. Tactical Integration:

- Implementing New Tactics: Introducing and ingraining his tactical philosophy into the team, which may take time for players to fully adapt to.

- Adapting to the Premier League: Adjusting tactics to cope with the unique challenges of the Premier League, including its pace and physicality.

Strategies for Overcoming Challenges

To navigate these obstacles successfully, Maresca can employ several strategies:

1. Building a Strong Backroom Staff:

- Experienced Team: Assembling a team of experienced and trusted assistants who can support in various aspects, from tactical analysis to player management.

- Specialized Coaches: Including coaches with specific expertise in areas such as set-pieces, fitness, and psychology to address all facets of team performance.

2. Effective Communication:

- Clear Vision and Goals: Communicating a clear vision and set of goals to the players, staff, and the broader club to ensure everyone is aligned.

- Regular Feedback: Maintaining open lines of communication with players, offering regular feedback, and addressing concerns proactively.

3. Balanced Rotation Policy:

- Squad Rotation: Implementing a balanced rotation policy to manage player fatigue and reduce the risk of injuries, ensuring key players remain fresh for crucial matches.

- Youth Integration: Gradually integrating young talents into the first team to provide depth and maintain squad morale.

4. Strategic Transfer Planning:

- Long-Term Recruitment: Focusing on long-term recruitment strategies that align with the club's philosophy and financial constraints.

- Data-Driven Decisions: Utilizing data analytics to make informed transfer decisions, ensuring that new signings fit into the tactical setup and long-term vision.

5. Tactical Flexibility:

- Adaptive Tactics: Being flexible with tactics, allowing for adjustments based on the opposition and match context to exploit weaknesses and maximize strengths.

- Continuous Learning: Staying updated with the latest tactical innovations and being willing to adapt and evolve the playing style as needed.

Long-Term Goals and Ambitions

Enzo Maresca's tenure at Chelsea is not only about achieving immediate success but also about establishing a foundation for sustained excellence. His long-term goals and ambitions include:

1. Establishing a Winning Culture:

- Sustained Success: Building a team capable of consistently competing for Premier League and Champions League titles.

- Instilling a Winning Mentality: Creating a culture where winning is embedded in the club's ethos, ensuring that players are motivated and driven to succeed in every competition.

2. Developing Homegrown Talent:

- Youth Academy Integration: Fostering a strong connection between the academy and the first team, ensuring a steady pipeline of talent.

- Player Development: Focusing on the holistic development of young players, preparing them to succeed at the highest levels.

3. Innovative Football:

- Tactical Evolution: Continually evolving the team's tactical approach to stay ahead of rivals and set new trends in football.

- Technology Integration: Leveraging the latest technology and data analytics to enhance training, performance, and decision-making.

4. Strengthening Club Identity:

- Philosophy and Style: Establishing a clear footballing philosophy and style of play that becomes synonymous with Chelsea.

- Global Brand: Enhancing Chelsea's brand globally through success on the pitch and engagement with fans around the world.

5. Sustainable Management:

- Financial Prudence: Operating within financial constraints to ensure long-term stability and compliance with regulations.

- Strategic Investments: Making strategic investments in facilities, staff, and infrastructure to support the club's growth.

6. Building Legacy:

- Enduring Impact: Aiming to leave a lasting legacy at Chelsea, not just in terms of trophies won, but also in the culture and structure of the club.

- Mentoring Future Leaders: Developing future leaders within the club, ensuring that the principles and values instilled during his tenure endure beyond his time at the club.

Enzo Maresca's appointment at Chelsea represents an exciting new chapter for both the manager and the club. By navigating potential challenges with strategic planning and a clear vision, Maresca can lead Chelsea to sustained success and cement his legacy as a top-tier manager.

Chapter 10: Legacy and Impact

Influence on Modern Football Tactics

Enzo Maresca's influence on modern football tactics is significant, particularly through his innovative approaches and his time working under Pep Guardiola at Manchester City. Here are key aspects of his tactical influence:

1. Possession-Based Play
2. High Press and Counter-Pressing
3. Versatility and Flexibility
4. Use of Data and Technology

Contributions to Coaching and Mentorship

Enzo Maresca's contributions to coaching and mentorship extend beyond his tactical prowess, influencing a new generation of football coaches and players. Key contributions include:

1. Mentoring Young Coaches:

- Development Programs: Maresca is actively involved in coaching development programs, sharing his knowledge and experiences with aspiring coaches. He often conducts workshops and seminars focusing on modern coaching methodologies.

- Influence: His journey from a player to a coach serves as an inspiring model for many young coaches looking to transition into management.

2. Player Development:

- Youth Integration: At Leicester City, Maresca demonstrated a keen eye for developing young talent, integrating academy players into the first team, and providing them with crucial playing time.

- Holistic Approach: His emphasis on not just tactical but also psychological and physical development has helped young players reach their full potential.

3. Building a Coaching Philosophy:

- Educational Initiatives: Maresca is known for his detailed approach to coaching, focusing on the minutiae of the game. He contributes to educational resources, including writing articles and participating in discussions that influence coaching practices globally.

- Legacy: His work at Manchester City's academy and with other youth setups has left a lasting impact on coaching standards and practices.

Lasting Legacy in the Football World

Enzo Maresca's legacy in the football world is shaped by his achievements, innovations, and contributions to the sport. His influence will be felt for years to come in various ways:

1. Tactical Innovator:

- Influence on Tactics: Maresca's tactical innovations, particularly his implementation of possession-based play and high pressing, have influenced many teams and coaches. His ability to blend tactical discipline with creative freedom sets a benchmark for modern football tactics.

2. Successful Manager:

- Championship Success: His success at Leicester City, particularly leading them to the Championship title and securing promotion to the Premier League, stands as a testament to his managerial capabilities.

- Future Prospects: As he continues his journey at Chelsea, his potential to achieve further success will add to his legacy, making him one of the most sought-after managers in the football world.

3. Mentorship and Development:

- Impact on Young Coaches: Maresca's mentorship has produced a ripple effect, influencing many young coaches who aspire to follow in his footsteps. His commitment to coaching education and player development will continue to inspire future generations.

- Player Legacies: The young talents he has nurtured and developed will carry forward his principles and methodologies, perpetuating his impact on the game.

4. Cultural Ambassador:

- Bridging Football Cultures: Maresca's career has seen him work across various football cultures, from Italy and Spain to England. His ability to adapt and succeed in different environments makes him a cultural ambassador for modern football.

Enzo Maresca's legacy and impact on football are multifaceted, spanning tactical innovation, coaching and mentorship, and lasting contributions to the sport. His journey is a testament to his dedication, intelligence, and passion for football, and his influence will undoubtedly shape the future of the game.

Appendix

Appendix

This appendix provides a comprehensive look at Enzo Maresca's managerial career, showcasing his statistical achievements and contributions to the clubs he has managed. The detailed breakdown highlights his successful strategies and his ability to adapt and thrive in various roles within the football management hierarchy.

Statistics and Records

Managerial Statistics (as of 2024)

Leicester City (2023-2024 Season)

- Total Matches: 53
- Wins: 36
- Draws: 4
- Losses: 13
- Points: 112
- Points per Match (PPM): 2.11

Competitions Breakdown:

- Championship:

- Matches: 46
- Wins: 31
- Draws: 4
- Losses: 11
- Points: 97
- PPM: 2.11

- FA Cup:
  - Matches: 4
  - Wins: 3
  - Losses: 1
  - Points: 9
  - PPM: 2.25
- EFL Cup:
  - Matches: 3
  - Wins: 2
  - Losses: 1
  - Points: 6
  - PPM: 2.00

Managerial Awards

- Championship Manager of the Month: Won 3 times during the 2023-2024 season

Previous Roles:
- Parma (2021-2022)
  - Matches: 14
  - Wins: 4
  - Draws: 5
  - Losses: 5
  - PPM: 1.21

- **Manchester City U23 (2020-2021)**
  - Matches: 28
  - Wins: 19
  - Draws: 6
  - Losses: 3
  - PPM: 2.21

Assistant Manager Roles:
- Manchester City (Assistant to Pep Guardiola, 2022-2023)

- West Ham United (Assistant to Manuel Pellegrini, 2018-2020)

- Sevilla FC (Technical Coach and Assistant, 2017-2018)

- Ascoli (Assistant Manager, 2017)

Managerial Highlights

Promotion to Premier League: Led Leicester City to win the Championship title in the 2023-2024 season.

Youth Development: Known for his success in developing young talents, particularly during his tenure at Manchester City's Elite Development Squad.